THE
SUCCESS
MESSAGES

Inspiration to Recharge

Your Passion, Potential & Purpose

By Romeo Marquez Jr.

The Success Messages

Copyright © 2013 by Romeo Marquez Jr.

ISBN-13: 978-0615950211
ISBN-10: 0615950213

Disclaimer

Printed in the United States of America

DEDICATED TO

YOU

May *The Success Messages* bring you greater joy, abundance, and happiness so that you serve the world with greater passion and purpose.

.

INTRODUCTION

One of the greatest treasures in life is the gift of inspiration. For me, inspiration comes in many ways: quotes, books, movies, stories, music, nature, and yes, even fortune cookies.

Inspiration, no matter where it comes from, elevates my spirit, expands my imagination, and ignites my vision to see greater possibilities in life.

IN THE BEGINNING

The messages you are about to read originated from my morning ritual, which consists of writing in my gratitude journal, meditation, visualization, prayer, and reading. This is a time where I cleanse my mind and recharge my spirit before I get swamped into life's busy schedule.

One of the great joys I experience during my morning ritual are the powerful conversations I have with God. It is usually during my meditations that He will whisper these simple yet profound sayings that awakens my spirit.

When I first began receiving these messages, I questioned my experience. I would ask myself, "Am I making this up or is this God really speaking to me?"

Over the next few days, more messages came pouring in and my curiosity grew stronger. Then I heard God say, "Trust that it is Me. I am here to guide you." After hearing those words again and again, my questioning eventually disappeared and soon enough I began surrendering to all that God was sharing with me.

These messages became so empowering for me that I decided to share them with other people by posting them on Facebook, Instagram, Twitter, and other social media sites. In doing so, I received tons of positive responses. People were saying things like, "Thank you so much for sharing this." "This is exactly what I needed to hear today." "I'm going to post this in my office."

It was so humbling to hear such kind words from my friends and colleagues. Their words inspired me so much that I knew I had to deliver these messages in a greater way. I knew it was time for me to compile them into a book. As such, the writing process began.

WITHIN THIS BOOK

In this book you will find a compilation of simple sayings that I call *The Success Messages*. These messages have been a great source of inspiration for me, and I hope they will do the same for you. Some of these teachings may connect with you and some may not. Some may connect with you at a later time. Whatever the case, my suggestion is that you receive what speaks to you most during this time of your life.

You will notice I added a *note* and an *affirmation* in addition to the message. The note serves as an extended thought to the teaching and the affirmation is there for you to personalize the teaching.

Speak the affirmations aloud so that you may embody the message. Feel it and say it with meaning. Post them on your desk, bathroom mirror, by your bed, or wherever you are most of the time. If you feel inspired to create your own affirmation, please do so.

This is no accident that this book has landed into your hands. It is here to serve a greater purpose and that purpose is to remind you of the greatness you have within you.

Thank you for taking the time to read this book of messages. I know that greater miracles are on their way. Keep believing and continue to trust in the process.

Believing in Your Greatness,
Romeo Marquez Jr.

The fulfillment of all dreams begin at the root of your imagination.

Note: *Please use wisely.*

Affirmation:

I take time to nurture my imagination so that I fulfill my dreams easily and effortlessly.

You are the *artist* as well as the *art* you create. There is no separation.

Note: *We are all artists in some form.*

Affirmation:

I am an artist who creates art to transform the world for the better.

Dreams are not wishes to be attained in the near future. They are imagined ideas meant to be lived right now.

Note: *Your ideas are needed now.*

Affirmation:

I say, "YES," to my dreams and choose to live them now.

What you say and do is the music to your imagination.

Note: *If you do not find joy and fulfillment to what you are playing, then you know it is time to orchestrate a new melody.*

Affirmation:

I am an instrument of God who orchestrates melodies that are fulfilling and joyful.

Your imagination is the biggest playground in the universe.

Note: *Do not let anything stop you from playing big.*

Affirmation:

I use my imagination to play
bigger than ever before.

Dance to the music of thy soul, for the world is your dance floor.

Note*: Dance freely without hesitation.*

Affirmation:

I dance freely to the music that plays within me.

Give yourself permission to take more time for your mission.

Note: *You help others by taking time for yourself.*

Affirmation:

I give myself permission to take more time for my mission so that I live a purposeful life.

Imagine your life. Then live your imagination.

Note: *Your imagination is infinite.*

Affirmation:

I use my imagination to create miracles in the world.

Inspirations that lie within are gifts designed specifically for you.

Note: *The gifts within you mean a lot more than you think.*

Affirmation:

I am designed with gifts to do great things.

Bless the world with your love
every single second.

Note: *B.L.E.S.S.- Bring Love Every
Single Second*

Affirmation:

I am a gift of love who blesses others with love.

Excuse all excuses that interfere
with your greatness.

Note: *Excuses are interferences to a
life you deserve.*

Affirmation:

I am living a life that I deserve filled with greatness.

God is putting together a few more things before your next BIG blessing.

Note*: Surrender and stay faithful.*

Affirmation:

I am patient and I surrender to God's perfect timing.

When God gives you a calling stop sending Him to voicemail.

Note: *Answer Him, for you are a big part of a miracle in the making.*

Affirmation:

I answer to the callings of God because I know miracles are on the way.

Do not let the ego get in the way,
for it erases God's opportunities.

Note: *E.G.O.- Erasing God's
Opportunities*

Affirmation:

I live with humility and
remain open to receiving God's
opportunities each and every day.

Your visions, talents, and gifts are signals for what you signed up for.

Note: *It is time to fully tap into your potential.*

Affirmation:

I use my visions, talents, and gifts as tools to make a greater difference in the world.

People see that you understand. People understand that you know. But people will really understand that you know when they see what you do.

Note: *Understanding is essential, but it is in the doing that creates the difference.*

Affirmation:

I do what I say and I do it to make a difference.

All that has been done unto you is the preparation for what is to come next for you.

Note: *Trust in the process, for it will make sense*

Affirmation:

I am equipped and prepared for all that comes my way.

For big dreams and ideas to flourish bring in God.

Note: *B.I.G.- Bring in God*

Affirmation:

I accomplish all great things with God.

Do not wander wondering the rest of your life.

Note: *Do wonders rather than wander.*

Affirmation:

I am created to do wonders for the world.

Harmonize with the tune God
sings within you.

Note: *Listen closely and align
yourself with the music.*

Affirmation:

I harmonize with the song God
plays within me.

Do not wait for opportunities.
Create opportunities.

Note: *Let the creation process begin.*

Affirmation:

I create opportunities that attract
greater opportunities.

Nurture the sign of excitement, for it is the re-fueling of the spirit.

Note: *Your excitement makes a difference.*

Affirmation:

I bring enthusiasm and excitement
in all that I do.

Resistance is the assistance for what is missing in your life.

Note: *Let go and go.*

Affirmation:

I have the power to overcome all
things that get in my way.

Just show up.

Note: *Your presence is a gift for others.*

Affirmation:

I am a gift to others when I show up.

Acting upon those inspired ideas is like giving the world a big hug.

Note: Hug big.

Affirmation:

I enjoy giving the world a big hug when I act upon those inspired ideas.

The heart is there to guide you.
The beat is to keep you moving.

Note: *Take a moment to listen to your heart.*

Affirmation:

I use my heart to guide me in the direction I am called to.

Set goals that move you to go out and live.

Note: *G.O.A.L.- Go Out And Live*

Affirmation:

My goals energize me to live more fully.

What you affirm becomes
the reality to your beingness.
Therefore, affirm that which you
desire for it shall become your
ultimate truth.

Note*: Affirm with power.*

Affirmation:

I am capable and well able to achieve all things with excellence.

Be not a waiter, but rather a server.

Note: *Waiting does not serve you.*

Affirmation:

I am here to serve with love and enthusiasm.

The actions of your distractions distant you from the actions of your destiny.

Note: *Only take actions that move you toward your destiny.*

Affirmation:

I take action on all things that bring me closer to my destiny.

When you do it now you have new opportunities waiting.

Note*: N.O.W.- New Opportunities Waiting*

Affirmation:

My actions bring in new and greater opportunities.

Those recent inspirations delivered
to you equal action.

Note: *I.D.E.A.- Inspirations
Delivered Equal Action*

Affirmation:

I act upon the inspirations that are coming to me.

Why are you pressing pause when God is pressing play?

Note: *Pressing pause does not serve your potential.*

Affirmation:

I step into my full potential by staying in sync with God.

Ideas replayed over and over again are whispers from God telling you it is time to get moving.

Note: *Bring God's whispers to life.*

Affirmation:

I move in the direction of God's whispers as soon as I hear them.

It is time to live in full expression.

Note: *L.I.F.E.- Live In Full Expression*

Affirmation:

I live my life and dreams in full expression.

Your mission is to move in service so that it operates now.

Note: M.I.S.S.I.O.N.- Movement in Service So It Operates Now

Affirmation:

I serve with a purpose that serves a greater purpose.

Love what you do and do it with love.

Note: *Do the things that bring you closer to love and joy.*

Affirmation:

I love all that I do and I do it all
with love.

Be ready for the gifts being presented, for they are God's inspirations for the soul.

Note: *G.I.F.T.S.- God's Inspirations For The Soul*

Affirmation:

I enjoy receiving all the gifts God is
sharing with me.

You are an infinite spirit created to do wonders.

Note: *You are capable of more than you think.*

Affirmation:

I am an infinite spirit that does wonders for the world.

Happiness arises the day you give it birth.

Note*: Your happiness brings more joy to the world.*

Affirmation:

I am filled with an abundance of happiness and pure joy.

Delays are a part of God's divine plan for the greater good.

Note: *G.O.O.D.- God Overcomes Our Delays*

Affirmation:

I surrender to God's perfect timing because I know it serves a greater purpose.

Let the storms in your life be dissipated through the light you shine upon others.

Note: *There will be storms. Just shine through.*

Affirmation:

I am filled with a light that radiates everywhere I go.

When you move inspiration repeatedly and celebrate love everyday, a miracle transpires.

Note: *M.I.R.A.C.L.E.- Moving Inspiration Repeatedly And Love Everyday*

Affirmation:

I create miracles with love everyday.

All endings are the creation to greater beginnings.

Note: *Something greater is on its way.*

Affirmation:

I am enjoying all the new miracles
God has placed into my life.

What lies between you and your next miracle may be the simple act of forgiveness.

Note: *Who do you need to forgive in your life in order to move forward?*

Affirmation:

I forgive all those who I know I need to forgive because I have been forgiven.

To get more done, do less with more effort.

Note: *Remember, less is more.*

Affirmation:

I put forth all my effort in all that I do.

There is a Divine blessing behind your every step.

Note: Walk with faith.

Affirmation:

I openly receive the blessings
behind my every step.

Your thoughts are the invitation to what you shall attract more of into your life.

Note: *Be mindful of the invitations you give out.*

Affirmation:

I use my thoughts to attract abundance and joy into my life.

When you realign yourself with God you become a greater blessing for others.

Note: *It is time for a re-alignment with God.*

Affirmation:

I realign myself with God to receive His blessings so that I can be a blessing for others.

All that you want shall arrive on time.

Note: Patience works in your favor.

Affirmation:

All that I attract arrives on time.

Focus on your mission rather than what is missing because what is missing does not keep you moving.

Note: Be mission-focused.

Affirmation:

I am equipped with all that I need to keep me moving toward my mission.

For a big miracle to show up in your life, be the miracle in someone else's.

Note*: Become the miracle.*

Affirmation:

I am a miracle that creates miracles
for others.

Detach from all that does not serve you.

Note*: Be around all things that do.*

Affirmation:

I surround myself with all things
that serve me and the greater good.

Work more on your discipline
rather than your distractions.

Note: *Distractions move you away.
Discipline brings you closer.*

Affirmation:

My discipline and focus are getting stronger and stronger everyday.

Take the time to quiet the mind.

Note: *It is in the silence that you shall hear God.*

Affirmation:

I take the time to listen closely to what God is sharing with me.

It will be your faith that brings about new possibilities.

Note: *Your faith is more powerful than you think.*

Affirmation:

My faith delivers new miracles into
the world.

You shall see more clearly when you close your eyes and connect with God.

Note: *Close your eyes and you shall see.*

Affirmation:

I take time to look inside to connect more with God.

Dreams come into fruition when you do right everyday and move.

Note: *D.R.E.A.M.- Do Right Everyday And Move*

Affirmation:

I live my dreams through movement and doing right everyday.

Let failure be the seeds to grow your faith to build a path for something greater.

Note: *Harvest your seeds with care.*

Affirmation:

I create a path of miracles with faith.

Do not let your fears interfere with your brilliance, for it is your "inner fear" that slows you down for what comes next.

Note: *Let your faith remove ALL fear.*

Affirmation:

I move with brilliance and
unshakable faith.

You are on the right track for your assignment.

Note: *Do not let others pull you away for what you have been assigned.*

Affirmation:

I am joyfully completing the assignment God has for me.

Your heart is the compass to life.

Note: *Let the heart guide you to your next arrival.*

Affirmation:

My heart knows exactly where I need to go.

God is proud of you.

Note*: Be proud of you.*

Affirmation:

I am grateful to be connected with a Source that appreciates me and loves me for who I am and all that I do.

It's time.

Note: *It always has been and always will be.*

Affirmation:

I step into my greatness to serve the greater good because I know it is time.

SOME FINAL WORDS

All that you have learned, decided, and experienced has led you to this very moment. What you choose to do today will determine the successes of your great future.

Remember this, life is about exploration and discoveries. It is filled with magic moments and many miracles. Yes, there will be challenges along the way, but in those challenges are breakthroughs that will produce greater changes in your life.

Continue to tap into the gifts and talents blessed within you and know that those ideas that flow through you are *The Success Message*s, you are destined to share with the world.

I look forward to experiencing all the miracles you are assigned to produce. I wish you major success, abundance, and super happiness.

Believing in Your Greatness,
Romeo Marquez Jr.

ACKNOWLEDGEMENTS

I would like to express major gratitude to all those who have come into my life and shared their presence with me. Thank you for inspiring me with your stories, gifts, and joy you bring to this world.

To Dad, thank you for being my a role model of hard work and determination in my life. Thank you for laughing with me and always loving me.

To Mom, thank you for being my role model of love and kindness and teaching me to love all people. Thank you for constantly cheering me on to achieve my dreams.

To Rowena Quianzon, thank you for being the best sister ever and for being a major positive role model in my life. I wouldn't be doing what I am doing if it wasn't for your encouragement and love through the years.

To Jennifer Redondo, thank you for believing in me. I am grateful for the unconditional love you bring into our relationship and for being my best friend, soul mate, and the love of my life. I am better because of you.

To Joseph Phillip Quianzon and my nephews (Moses, Noah, Jacob, and Isaac), for strengthening my faith and expanding my imagination.

To Jack Canfield, thank you for your mentorship and being a guiding light to elevate my consciousness. Your love and teachings have empowered me to live my life with greater purpose and passion while making a positive difference around the world. I am grateful to be on this transformational journey with you.

To the Canfield Training Group team, Breakthrough to Success Family, and Train the Trainer Family, your love and the miracles you create in the world inspires me every single day. Thank you all for doing what you do.

To all my friends and family, thank you for your constant love and support. Thank you for cheering me on with your encouraging words and loving spirit. I continue to inspire others because all of you continue to inspire me.

To all my fans and audiences who I had the honor to share my story and teachings with, your presence means so much to me more than you know. Your love and kind words remind me to never give up.

To God, thank You. Thank You for giving me the vision to see the miracle in all people. Thank You for giving me a voice to express love and joy to inspire others. Thank You for Your guidance every step of the way. It's been a long journey, but with You *all* things are possible. Thank You.

ABOUT THE AUTHOR

ROMEO MARQUEZ JR. is a sought-after international motivational speaker, transformational trainer, and success coach who has delivered more than 1,000 presentations to over 200,000 audience members worldwide covering topics of Leadership, Motivation, Effective Communication, Team Building, Video Marketing, and Presentation Skills. He works with celebrities, business professionals, educators, and students to maximize their potential so they may live a life with purpose and passion.

From speaking on the TEDx platform in India to performing his inspirational one-man show, *"It's Time,"* in Las Vegas and New York, Romeo's diverse talent in the field of personal and professional development with a mission to making a positive difference has made him a favorite speaker and trainer among many organizations and conferences.

Romeo earned his B.A. Degree from UCLA's Theatre, Film & Television School and has trained with an elite group of global success leaders personally invited by Jack Canfield, best-selling author and co-creator of *"Chicken Soup for the Soul"* series.

As a professor for theatre, film & television and member of the National Speakers Association as well as the Screen Actors Guild, Romeo continues to expand his journey with enthusiasm and love to be of service to help all humanity for the universal good.

To learn more about Romeo, visit:

www.RomeoMarquezJr.com

Connect with him on Social Media:

www.Facebook.com/RomeoMarquezJr

www.YouTube.com/RomeoMarquezJr

www.Twitter.com/RomeoMarquezJr

www.Instagram.com/RomeoMarquezJr

Looking for a Professional Speaker for your Upcoming Event?

"Working with Romeo Marquez Jr. has been an absolute pleasure, as his vision, passion, and commitment to making a positive difference in the world, is **SECOND TO NONE.***"*

~JACK CANFIELD, Co-Creator of the
#1 New York Times Best-Selling book series "Chicken Soup for the Soul" and "The Success Principles"

Recognized by organizations worldwide as one of the most engaging and captivating speakers and trainers, Romeo shares a system of success principles that cover topics of *Motivation, Goal-Setting, Leadership, Team Building, Effective Communication, and Presentation Skills.*

Available for:

Conference Keynotes, Leadership Programs, Public Seminars, Colleges & Universities, Youth Conferences, School Assemblies

To invite Romeo Marquez Jr. to speak at your next event, or schedule a success coaching session with him, contact:

510-629-9564   Booking@RomeoMarquezJr.com

RECOMMENDED READINGS

The following is a list of recommended books that will enhance **The Success Messages** so that you produce the extraordinary results you are destined to achieve (and more):

THE SUCCESS PRINCIPLES, *by Jack Canfield and Janet Switzer*

THE KEY TO LIVING THE LAW OF ATTRACTION, *by Jack Canfield and D.D Watkins*

INSPIRATION, *by Dr. Wayne W. Dyer*

10 SECRETS FOR SUCCESS AND INNER PEACE, *Dr. Wayne W. Dyer*

SUCCESS THROUGH A POSITIVE MENTAL ATTITUDE, *by Napoleon Hill and W. Clement Stone*

HOW SUCCESSFUL PEOPLE THINK, *by John C. Maxwell*

AS A MAN THINKETH, *by James Allen*

YOUR BEST LIFE NOW, *by Joel Osteen*

LETTERS TO THE UNCHURCHED, *by J.P. Quianzon*

THE POWER OF POSITIVE THINKING, *by Norman Vincent Peale*

THE MAGIC OF THINKING BIG, *by David Schwartz*

THE SECRET, *by Rhonda Byrne*

Discounts available for multiple copies of
The Success Messages. For more details, email us at
Books@RomeoMarquezJr.com.

May *The Success Messages* bring you greater joy, abundance, and fulfillment so that you serve the world with greater love.

It's Time.

To experience more, visit:
www.RomeoMarquezJr.com

www.ingramcontent.com/pod-product-compliance
Lightning Source LLC
Chambersburg PA
CBHW072004060426
42446CB00042B/1818